KIA O MATE!

Welcome to "Sweet As! Kiwi Slangs, Words & Phrases: A Mini Illustrated Dictionary," your passport to the vibrant and sometimes baffling world of New Zealand slang. If you've ever found yourself scratching your head at a Kiwi conversation, wondering if they're speaking English or some secret code, then this book is for you!

We'll take you on a hilarious journey through the everyday lingo, quirky expressions, and downright bonkers phrases that make up the Kiwi vernacular. From "chur" to "choice" and "hard yakka" to "munted," we've got you covered.

Think of this book as your trusty sidekick, ready to translate Kiwi-isms into plain English, and equip you with the lingo to blend in like a local (or at least have a good laugh trying!).

How to use this book:

- Flick through the pages and marvel at the colourful illustrations.
- Sound out the words with our handy pronunciation guides (no more awkward mispronunciations!).
- Chuckle at the example sentences and imagine yourself using these phrases in real life.
- Test your newfound knowledge with the quizzes and puzzles sprinkled throughout.
- Most importantly, have a bloody good laugh and embrace the Kiwi way of life!

So, whether you're planning a trip to Aotearoa, want to impress your Kiwi mates, or simply love learning about different cultures, grab a cuppa, settle in, and get ready to unlock the secrets of Kiwi slang!

Chur, and happy reading!

GIDDAY
gih-DAY

WHAT IT MEANS

A casual and friendly way to say "hello."

HOW TO USE IT

"Gidday, mate! How's it going?"

KIA ORA
kee aw-RAH

WHAT IT MEANS

A formal greeting in Māori, also used casually.

HOW TO USE IT

"Kia ora, welcome to our home!"

HOWZIT GOIN'?
howz it GO-in

WHAT IT MEANS

A common way to ask someone how they are doing.

HOW TO USE IT

"Hey, howzit goin'? Haven't seen you in ages!"

WOTCHA?
wotch-UH

WHAT IT MEANS

Casual greeting, similar to "what's happening?"

HOW TO USE IT

"Wotcha, mate? Fancy a pint?"

CHUR
churr

WHAT IT MEANS

Thanks, cheers, or a general greeting.

HOW TO USE IT

"Chur for the help, bro!" or "Chur, see you later!"

SWEET AS
sweet az

WHAT IT MEANS

An expression of approval or agreement, meaning "great."

HOW TO USE IT

"That concert was sweet as!"

CHOICE
choyce

WHaT iT MeaNS

Another way to say "excellent" or "great."

HOW TO USe iT

"That fish and chips was choice!"

BRO/CUZ
bro / cuz

WHAT IT MEANS

Informal terms of address for a friend or mate.

HOW TO USE IT

"Hey bro, catch you later!"

SHE'LL BE RIGHT
sheel bee RIGHT

WHAT IT MEANS

A laid-back expression meaning "it will be okay."

HOW TO USE IT

"Don't stress about the rain, she'll be right."

NO WORRIES
no WURR-eez

WHAT IT MEANS

A common response meaning "no problem."

HOW TO USE IT

"Thanks for the lift!" "No worries, mate."

CHEERS

CHEERS

WHAT IT MEANS

Can be used as both a greeting and a farewell.

HOW TO USE IT

"Cheers, mate, see you around!"

LATERS
LAY-tuhz

WHaT iT MeaNS

A shortened, casual way to say "see you later."

HOW TO USe iT

"Laters, I'm off to the beach!"

EXPRESSING EMOTIONS

STOKED
STOHKED

WHAT IT MEANS

Excited, happy

HOW TO USE IT

"I'm so stoked about the upcoming concert!"

AMPED
AMPT

WHAT IT MEANS

Excited, energetic

HOW TO USE IT

"We're all amped up for the rugby game tonight!"

BUZZING
BUZZ-ing

WHAT IT MEANS

Excited, thrilled

HOW TO USE IT

"The crowd was buzzing after the All Blacks' victory!"

CHUFFED
CHUFFED

WHAT IT MEANS

Pleased, happy

HOW TO USE IT

"I'm chuffed to bits with my new car!"

MINT

MINT

WHAT IT MEANS

Awesome, great

HOW TO USE IT

"That surf session was mint!"

CRACK UP
KRACK UP

WHaT iT MeaNS

To find something hilarious or funny

HOW TO USe iT

"His jokes always crack me up!"

GOOD ON YA
GOOD on yuh

WHAT IT MEANS

An expression of praise or congratulations

HOW TO USE IT

"You aced the exam? Good on ya, mate!"

GUTTED
GUTT-ed

WHAT IT MEANS

Extremely disappointed or upset

HOW TO USE IT

"I was gutted when my team lost the final."

BUMMED

BUMMED

WHAT IT MEANS

Disappointed or sad

HOW TO USE IT

"I'm feeling a bit bummed about the weather cancelling our picnic."

MUNTED
MUN-ted

WHAT IT MEANS

Broken, damaged, or in a bad state

HOW TO USE IT

"My bike got munted after that crash."

KNACKERED
NACK-uhd

WHaT iT MeaNS

Tired, exhausted

HOW TO use iT

"I'm absolutely knackered after that hike."

BUGGER
BUG-uh

WHAT IT MEANS

An exclamation of frustration, annoyance, or surprise

HOW TO USE IT

"Bugger! I left my keys at home!"

TAKING THE PISS
TAY-king the PISS

WHAT IT MEANS

Teasing or making fun of someone in a lighthearted way

HOW TO USE IT

"He's always taking the piss out of my accent, but it's all good fun."

DODGY
DODGE-ee

WHAT IT MEANS

Suspicious, unreliable, or of questionable quality

HOW TO USE IT

"That food stall looks a bit dodgy, let's eat somewhere else."

YEAH NAH
yeh NAH

WHAT IT MEANS

A way to say "no" that can also soften the rejection or express uncertainty.

HOW TO USE IT

"Want to go to the movies?" "Yeah nah, I'm feeling a bit tired tonight."

NAH YEAH
NAH yeh

WHAT IT MEANS

A way to say "yes" that can also express agreement with a slight hesitation or reservation.

HOW TO USE IT

"Did you enjoy the concert?" "Nah yeah, it was alright."

EH?

ay

WHAT IT MEANS

Used at the end of a sentence to seek confirmation or agreement.

HOW TO USE IT

"Beautiful day, eh?"

HARD CASE
HARD KAYSE

WHAT IT MEANS

Someone who is funny, a bit eccentric, or has a strong personality.

HOW TO USE IT

"My uncle is a real hard case, always telling jokes and stories."

GOOD AS GOLD

good az GOLD

WHAT IT MEANS

Excellent, perfect

HOW TO USE IT

"The weather's good as gold today!"

NO DRAMAS

no DRAH-mas

WHAT IT MEANS

No problem, no worries

HOW TO USE IT

"Forgot your wallet? No dramas, I'll shout you."

CHOICE AS

CHOYCE az

WHAT IT MEANS

Really good, excellent

HOW TO USE IT

"That pie was choice as!"

BUGGER ALL

BUG-ger all

WHAT IT MEANS

Nothing at all

HOW TO USE IT

"There's bugger all to do around here."

HARD YAKKA

HARD YAK-kuh

WHAT IT MEANS

Hard work

HOW TO USE IT

"Digging that hole was hard yakka."

SMOKO

SMOH-koh

WHAT IT MEANS

A break from work, often for a cigarette or snack

HOW TO USE IT

"Time for smoko!"

UP THE DUFF

up the DUFF

WHAT IT MEANS

Pregnant

HOW TO USE IT

"She's up the duff with her second child."

FULL OF BEANS

full of BEENS

WHAT IT MEANS

Energetic, lively

HOW TO USE IT

"The kids are full of beans today."

NOT EVEN

not EE-vun

WHAT iT MEANS

Absolutely not, no way

HOW TO USE iT

"Are you going to bungy jump?" "Not even!"

CHUCK A SICKIE

CHUCK uh SICK-ee

WHaT iT MeaNS

Take a day off work when you're not actually sick

HOW TO USe iT

"I think I'll chuck a sickie tomorrow and go to the beach."

CRACK A FATTY

KRACK uh FAT-tee

WHAT IT MEANS

Open a can of beer

HOW TO USE IT

"Let's crack a fatty and watch the game."

SPIT THE DUMMY

SPIT the DUM-mee

WHAT IT MEANS

Have a tantrum, get upset

HOW TO USE IT

"He spat the dummy when he didn't get his way."

HE'S GOT TICKETS ON HIMSELF

heez got TICK-its on him-SELF

WHAT IT MEANS

He has a high opinion of himself, he's arrogant.

HOW TO USE IT

"He thinks he's the best at everything. He's definitely got tickets on himself."

AWAY WITH THE FAIRIES

uh-WAY with the FAIR-eez

WHAT IT MEANS

Daydreaming, not paying attention.

HOW TO USE IT

"She's staring out the window, away with the fairies again."

LIKE A SHAG ON A ROCK

like uh SHAG on uh ROCK

WHAT IT MEANS

Alone, isolated.

HOW TO USE IT

"I felt like a shag on a rock when everyone else left the party early."

UP THE CREEK WITHOUT A PADDLE

up the CREEK with-OUT uh PAD-dul

WHAT IT MEANS

In a difficult situation with no easy solution.

HOW TO USE IT

"We lost our map and our phones are dead. We're up the creek without a paddle."

DON'T GET YOUR KNICKERS IN A KNOT

downt get yor NICK-erz in uh NOT

WHAT IT MEANS

Don't get upset or stressed.

HOW TO USE IT

"Don't get your knickers in a knot over the traffic, we'll get there eventually."

ALL OVER IT LIKE A RASH

all OH-ver it like uh RASH

WHAT IT MEANS

Enthusiastically tackling a task or situation.

HOW TO USE IT

"She's all over it like a rash, organizing the whole event in no time."

HAPPY AS LARRY

HAP-pee az LAR-ree

WHAT IT MEANS

Very happy, content.

HOW TO USE IT

"She's been happy as Larry ever since she got that new job."

WOULDN'T SHOUT IF A SHARK BIT HIM

WOOD-int SHOUT if uh SHARK bit im

WHAT IT MEANS

Stingy, unwilling to spend money.

HOW TO USE IT

"Don't expect him to buy you a drink, he wouldn't shout if a shark bit him."

LIKE A DOG WITH TWO TAILS

like uh DOG with two TAYLZ

WHAT IT MEANS

Very happy, excited.

HOW TO USE IT

"He was like a dog with two tails when he found
out he'd won the lottery."

BETTER THAN A POKE IN THE EYE WITH A BURNT STICK

BET-tuh than uh POHK in the
EYE with uh burnt STICK

WHAT IT MEANS

Better than nothing, a small consolation.

HOW TO USE IT

"At least we didn't lose the game completely.
It's better than a poke in the eye with a burnt
stick, I guess."

CHIPPIES
CHIP-eez

WHAT IT MEANS

French fries/Potato chips

HOW TO USE IT

"Can I get a burger with a side of chippies, please?"

L & P
ell 'n' PEE

WHaT iT MeaNS

Lemon & Paeroa, a iconic New Zealand soft drink

HOW TO USe iT

"Nothing beats a cold L&P on a hot summer day."

PAVLOVA
pav-LOH-vuh

WHAT IT MEANS

Meringue-based dessert topped with whipped cream and fresh fruit

HOW TO USE IT

"Pavlova is a classic Kiwi dessert, perfect for sharing."

PINEAPPLE LUMPS
PYNE-appl lumps

WHAT iT MeaNS

Chocolate-covered pineapple candy

HOW TO USe iT

"Pineapple lumps are a sweet Kiwi treat."

HOKEY POKEY ICE CREAM
HOH-kee POH-kee

WHAT IT MEANS

Vanilla ice cream with honeycomb toffee pieces

HOW TO USE IT

"Hokey pokey is my all-time favorite ice cream flavor."

FISH AND CHIPS
FISH and CHIPS

WHAT IT MEANS

Take-away meal of battered or crumbed fish
served with hot chips (fries)

HOW TO USE IT

"Let's grab some fish and chips for dinner
tonight."

PIE
PIE

WHAT IT MEANS

Savory meat pie, often eaten as a snack or lunch

HOW TO USE IT

"I'm popping down to the dairy for a pie."

CUPPA
CUP-uh

WHAT IT MEANS

A cup of tea

HOW TO USE IT

"Fancy a cuppa and a biscuit?"

BREW
BROO

WHAT IT MEANS

Beer

HOW TO USE IT

"I'm heading to the pub for a brew with the lads."

COLDIE
COL-dee

WHAT IT MEANS

A cold beer

HOW TO USE IT

"It's a scorcher today, I could really go for a coldie."

BYO
bee-wy-OH

WHaT iT MeaNS

Bring Your Own (alcohol)

HOW TO USe iT

"The party is BYO, so don't forget to grab some beers on the way."

SHOUTING A ROUND
SHOW-ting uh ROUND

WHAT IT MEANS

Buying a round of drinks for everyone in your group

HOW TO USE IT

"It's my turn to shout a round at the pub tonight."

SOCIAL ACTIVITIES

FLATTING
FLAT-ing

WHAT IT MEANS

Sharing an apartment or house with friends

HOW TO USE IT

"I'm flatting with a couple of mates from uni."

HANGING OUT
HANG-ing OUT

WHAT IT MEANS

Spending time relaxing or socializing with friends

HOW TO USE IT

"We're just hanging out at the beach today."

GOING FOR A DRIVE/HOON

GO-ing for a DRIVE/HOON

WHaT iT MeaNS

Going for a leisurely drive (drive) or a fast, exciting drive (hoon)

HOW TO USe iT

"Let's go for a hoon up the coast this weekend!"

HAVING A YARN

HAV-ing a YARN

WHAT IT MEANS

Having a chat or conversation

HOW TO USE IT

"We had a good yarn over a cuppa this morning."

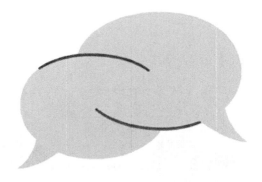

WATCHING THE FOOTY

WATCH-ing the FOOT-ee

WHaT iT MeaNS

Watching rugby, or sometimes other sports like
football or cricket

HOW TO USe iT

"The whole country will be watching the footy
when the All Blacks play."

NATURE & OUTDOOR

BUSH
bush

WHAT IT MEANS

Native forest or wilderness area

HOW TO USE IT

"We're going for a hike in the bush this weekend."

BACH
batch

WHAT IT MEANS

A small, often rustic holiday home or cabin

HOW TO USE IT

"We're spending the summer at our bach by the lake."

WOP-WOPS
wop-wops

WHAT IT MEANS

A remote, isolated area

HOW TO USE IT

"He lives out in the wop-wops, miles from anywhere."

THE 'NAKI
thuh NACK-ee

WHAT IT MEANS

Taranaki, a region known for its volcanic cone,
Mt. Taranaki

HOW TO USE IT

"I'm heading up to The 'Naki for a surf trip."

THE MOUNT
thuh MOUNT

WHAT IT MEANS

Mount Maunganui, a popular beach town with a distinctive mountain

HOW TO USE IT

"The Mount is a great spot for a summer holiday."

MAINLAND
MAYN-land

WHAT IT MEANS

The South Island of New Zealand

HOW TO USE IT

"We're taking the ferry across to the Mainland next week."

SUNNIES
SUN-eez

WHAT IT MEANS

Sunglasses

HOW TO USE IT

"Don't forget your sunnies, it's going to be a
bright day."

JANDALS
JAN-duls

WHAT IT MEANS

Flip-flops/thongs

HOW TO USE IT

"Chuck on your jandals and let's head to the beach."

SOUTHERLY BUSTER

SUTH-er-lee BUST-er

WHAT IT MEANS

A cold, strong wind from the south

HOW TO USE IT

"The southerly buster is making it feel much colder today."

SUNBLOCK
SUN-block

WHAT IT MEANS

Sunscreen

HOW TO USE IT

"Slip, slop, slap! Don't forget to put on some sunblock."

MOZZIE

MOZZ-ee

WHAT IT MEANS

Mosquito

HOW TO USE IT

"The mozzies are out in force tonight!"

SCORCHER
SCORE-cher

WHAT IT MEANS

A very hot day

HOW TO USE IT

"It's a scorcher today, make sure you stay hydrated."

KIWIS

KEE-weez

WHAT IT MEANS

Flightless birds, also a nickname for New Zealanders

HOW TO USE IT

"We saw some kiwis at the wildlife sanctuary!"

Gidday, mate!

PENGUINS
PENG-wins

WHAT IT MEANS

Various species of penguins found in New Zealand

HOW TO USE IT

"The little blue penguins are so cute!"

TUATARA
too-uh-TAR-uh

WHAT IT MEANS

A unique reptile endemic to New Zealand

HOW TO USE IT

"The tuatara is a living fossil, it's amazing!"

KEA
KEE-uh

WHAT IT MEANS

A cheeky and intelligent alpine parrot

HOW TO USE IT

"The kea are known for their mischievous antics, like stealing car parts!"

WEKA
WEE-kuh

WHAT IT MEANS

A flightless bird known for its curiosity and scavenging habits

HOW TO USE IT

"Watch out for the weka, they'll try to snatch your food!"

PUKEKO
poo-KEH-koh

WHAT IT MEANS

A colorful swamp bird with long legs

HOW TO USE IT

"The pukeko are often seen foraging in paddocks."

TRAMPING
TRAMP-ing

WHAT IT MEANS

Hiking or backpacking, often for multiple days

HOW TO USE IT

"We're going tramping in the Abel Tasman
National Park next week."

DOC

DOC

WHaT iT MeaNS

Department of Conservation, the government agency responsible for conservation

HOW TO USe iT

"Make sure you check the DoC website for track conditions before you go."

HUT

HUT

WHAT IT MEANS

A basic shelter for hikers and trampers

HOW TO USE IT

"We'll be staying in a DoC hut overnight on our tramp."

SCROGGIN
SCROG-in

WHAT IT MEANS

Trail mix, a snack mix of nuts, seeds, and dried fruit

HOW TO USE IT

"Don't forget to pack some scroggin for energy on the hike."

PACK
PACK

WHAT IT MEANS

Backpack

HOW TO USE IT

"Make sure your pack is well-adjusted for comfort on the trail."

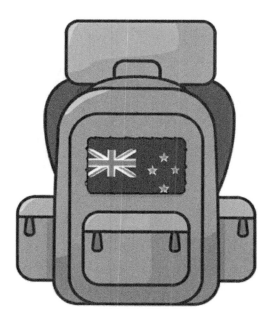

CHUCKING A LINE IN
CHUCK-ing uh LINE in

WHAT IT MEANS

Going fishing

HOW TO USE IT

"I'm heading down to the river to chuck a line in this afternoon."

WHITEBAIT
WHITE-bait

WHAT IT MEANS

Small, translucent fish, considered a delicacy

HOW TO USE IT

"Whitebait fritters are a real Kiwi treat."

KOURA

KOH-ra

WHAT IT MEANS

Freshwater crayfish

HOW TO USE IT

"We're going to try and catch some koura in the stream today."

SNAPPER
SNAP-puh

WHAT IT MEANS

A popular saltwater fish

HOW TO USE IT

"Snapper is my favorite fish to catch and eat."

MŌRENA

MOH-reh-nuh

WHAT IT MEANS

Good morning (formal)

HOW TO USE IT

"Mōrena, how are you today?"

MARAE

muh-RYE

WHaT iT MeaNS

Meeting house, central to Māori communities, a place of gathering and ceremony

HOW TO USe iT

"The marae is a sacred place where we welcome visitors and hold events."

HĀNGĪ

HAHNG-ee

WHAT IT MEANS

Traditional Māori feast cooked in an earth oven

HOW TO USE IT

"The hāngī was delicious, especially the tender meat and vegetables."

ATA MĀRIE

AH-tah MA-ree-eh

WHAT IT MEANS

Good morning (informal)

HOW TO USE IT

"Ata mārie, cuz! Ready for a swim?"

NGĀ MIHI

NAH mee-hee

WHAT IT MEANS

Best wishes/regards

HOW TO USE IT

"Ngā mihi to your whānau."

HAERE RĀ

HIGH-reh rah

WHAT IT MEANS

Goodbye (to someone leaving)

HOW TO USE IT

"Haere rā, safe travels!"

E NOHO RĀ

Eh NO-hoh rah

WHAT IT MEANS

Goodbye (to someone staying)

HOW TO USE IT

"E noho rā, I'll see you soon!"

WHĀNAU

FAH-now

WHAT IT MEANS

Family, extended family, or a close-knit group

HOW TO USE IT

"My whānau is coming over for a barbecue this weekend."

MANA

MAH-nah

WHAT IT MEANS

Prestige, authority, respect, power

HOW TO USE IT

"He is a respected leader with great mana."

TAPU

TAH-poo

WHAT IT MEANS

Sacred, restricted, prohibited

HOW TO USE IT

"Certain areas of the marae are tapu and should not be entered by visitors."

NOA

NOH-ah

WHaT iT MeaNS

Ordinary, unrestricted, free from tapu

HOW TO USe iT

"Once the ceremony is over, the food becomes noa and everyone can eat."

KAITIAKITANGA

KAI-tee-ah-kee-TANG-ah

WHAT IT MEANS

Guardianship, stewardship, the responsibility to care for the environment

HOW TO USE IT

"Kaitiakitanga is a core value in Māori culture, promoting sustainable practices."

TANGI

TAHNG-ee

WHAT IT MEANS

Funeral, a time of mourning and remembrance

HOW TO USE IT

"The tangi was a moving tribute to his life."

Printed in Great Britain
by Amazon